POCKET MANUAL
PREDATORS

This updated edition published in July 2020
previously published in 2007

British Library Cataloguing-in-Publication Data:
A catalogue record for this book is available from the British Library

ISBN 978 1 78521 728 9

Library of Congress catalog card no. 2019957234

Published by Haynes Publishing,
Sparkford, Yeovil, Somerset BA22 7JJ, UK
Tel: +44 (0)1963 440635
Website: www.haynes.com

Haynes North America, Inc.,
859 Lawrence Drive, Newbury Park, California 91320, USA

Printed and bound in China

All photographs courtesy iSto
Alamy; pp14/15, 15 bottom rig
50/51, 52/53, 58/59, 64/65, 6
116/117, 118/119, 127 top, 143
Getty; pp27, 36/37, 38/39, 48
Photolibrary; pp39 bottom lef
SeaPics; pp51 top left, 162/16

POCKET MANUAL
PREDATORS

Haynes

Contents

Now read the book!

This exciting book features 45 of the world's deadliest predators, from big cats such as the Asiatic lion and Siberian tiger and underwater menaces like the electric eel and red-bellied piranha to the fearsome goliath birdeater spider and the enormous Komodo dragon. Packed with fascinating facts, stunning photographs and all the vital statistics, this is the essential pocket guide.

American
Alligator
The alligator that gets a bit snappy

American
Alligator

The alligator that gets a bit snappy

The American alligator is a formidable predator. They spend most of their time in wetlands and swim quickly in water. Despite being slow-moving on land, these alligators can still manage short bursts of up to 48kph! The tail makes up half the alligator's total body length and is used for swimming or as a defence weapon when the alligator feels threatened. They feed mostly on fish, birds, mammals, turtles and amphibians. However, larger alligators have been known to attack cattle, panthers and bears. In fact, any animal living in or near the water becomes potential prey to this hungry creature. They are at the top of their food chain and don't have any predators, apart from man. They use their large, strong jaws to capture, crush and dismember prey. Despite having about 80 teeth, alligators can't chew, so instead their stomach contains little stones to help grind up their food. These are certainly necessary, as alligators swallow their victims whole!

Statistics

Latin name:	*Alligator mississippiensis*
Also known as:	N/a
Distribution:	South-eastern America
Habitat:	Wetlands
Average size:	4–4.5m
Average weight:	450kg
Number of offspring:	20–50 eggs
Population:	Unknown
Life span:	30 years

American
Black Vulture

The bird that keeps its eyes open

American
Black Vulture

The bird that keeps its eyes open

Vultures are classified into two groups – Old World and New World vultures. The American black vulture belongs to the latter, and is a large bird of prey with an excellent sense of smell. They are scavenging birds that feed mainly on dead animal carcasses (carrion). However, they are opportunistic predators and will feast on any suitable food source, also preying on new-born, wounded or sick wild animals (and occasionally, domestic animals, too), taking advantage of their defenceless state. They forage in groups but also soar high in search of food. When airborne, they keep their eyes open for other vultures swooping down low – which is a key sign that they have spotted food. They are aggressive and dominant birds, and will fight and scare off other scavengers to enjoy a meal in relative peace. They can also eat rotten flesh that may contain bacteria, as these are destroyed in their stomachs.

Statistics

Latin name:	*Coragyps atratus*
Also known as:	N/a
Distribution:	North and South America
Habitat:	Open habitats
Average size:	65cm long (1.5m wingspan)
Average weight:	1.5kg
Number of offspring:	2–3 eggs
Population:	Unknown
Life span:	5 years

Asiatic
Lion
The big cat with a big pounce

Asiatic
Lion
The big cat with a big pounce

Lions are the second largest feline species after the tiger but are the most powerful hunters. The Asiatic lion is a subspecies found only in India. Known as Lord of the Beasts or King of the Jungle they are the only cats to live in prides. They feed on wild pigs, cattle, antelope and deer. Lionesses usually hunt in packs by night or at dawn, and the males rarely take part. Asiatic lions will stalk prey, carefully approaching, before charging at it and either grabbing it or knocking it down before it outruns them. Although they can reach speeds of 80kph they tire easily, hence the need to get up close before giving chase. Lionesses will also work together on a hunt, as one lioness drives prey towards a bigger group lying in wait, ready to attack. Few animals survive a lion attack, as they are very short and powerful and almost always kill by using strangulation.

Statistics

Latin name:	*Panthera leo persica*
Also known as:	**Indian lion**
Distribution:	**Gir Forest, India**
Habitat:	**Forests**
Average size:	**2m long**
Average weight:	**100–225kg**
Number of offspring:	**1–6 cubs**
Population:	**About 350**
Life span:	**12–18 years in the wild**

Black Widow
Spider
The eight-legged monster

Black Widow
Spider
The eight-legged monster

The name 'black widow' usually refers to the three North American species. They are extremely poisonous arachnids – their venom is 15 times as poisonous as that of a rattlesnake. They are found throughout the world and are renowned for their neurotoxic venom (a potent toxin that affects nerve cells). They prey on a whole host of insects but occasionally feed on other arachnids, too. They cast their web and wait until prey entangles itself within it. The spider then quickly comes out of its hiding place, wraps its victim securely in its strong web, then punctures and poisons its prey. The spider keeps a tight grip on its victim, as the venom gradually takes effect – usually about 10 minutes. When movement of its victim ceases, digestive enzymes are released into the wound, before the black widow spider carries its prey back to its hiding place to feed on it.

Statistics

Latin name:	*Latrodectus mactans*
Also known as:	N/a
Distribution:	All over the world, especially North America
Habitat:	Dark places, such as under logs or rocks
Average size:	Up to 2.5cm
Average weight:	Unknown
Number of offspring:	4–9 egg sacs, each containing 100–400 eggs
Population:	Unknown
Life span:	Up to 5 years

Box
Jellyfish
The marine stinger

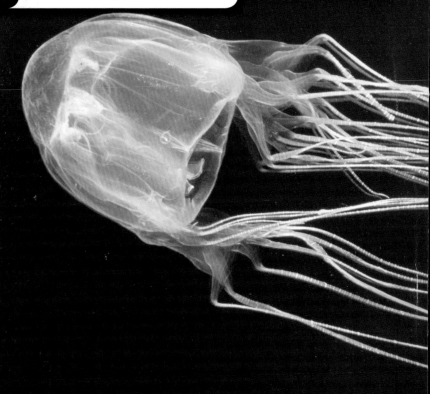

Box
JellyFish
The marine stinger

Chironex fleckeri is a highly venomous species of box jellyfish, which are water-dwelling invertebrates that belong to the class of Cubozoa. They are known for the often-fatal effects of their venom, which is one of the most powerful and deadly in the animal kingdom – it has caused more than 5,000 deaths since the 1800s. They have a complex system of 24 eyes on the centre of each side of their bell, some of which may even be able to form images – though this hasn't been scientifically proven yet. When moving flat out, they can reach speeds of up to 1.8m per second (about 6.5kph), as they shoot along in a jet-like motion. Some box jellyfish hunt their prey using this motion, rather than drifting like most jellyfish do. Their venom is used to stun and kill prey, such as invertebrates and small fish, prior to eating, but it is also used for defence against predators.

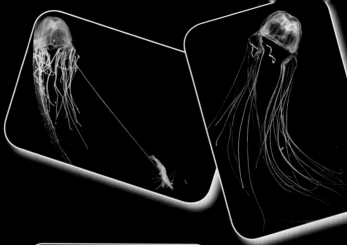

Statistics

Latin name:	*Chironex fleckeri*
Also known as:	Box fish, sea wasp or marine stinger
Distribution:	Australia, the Philippines and other tropical areas
Habitat:	Oceans and seas
Average size:	18cm along each side of the bell, up to 15 tentacles on each corner
Average weight:	Unknown
Number of offspring:	N/a
Population:	Unknown
Life span:	Unknown

Cane
Toad
The toad with a nasty taste

Cane
Toad
The toad with a nasty taste

Cane toads are warty amphibians, with horned ridges on their heads. Their skin is incredibly poisonous, the most venomous part being on its shoulders. If attacked, this toad will ooze milky-white venom into its predator's mouth, so they are highly toxic to most animals if eaten. Cane toads are omnivorous, nocturnal creatures that forage and feed, locating their prey by movement or using their sense of smell. They are ground-dwelling predators that are not fussy eaters and tend to eat anything they can swallow, hence their large size! They prey mainly on insects but have been known to eat small snakes, frogs, lizards, mice and even dog food from a bowl! On occasion, they also eat their own young.

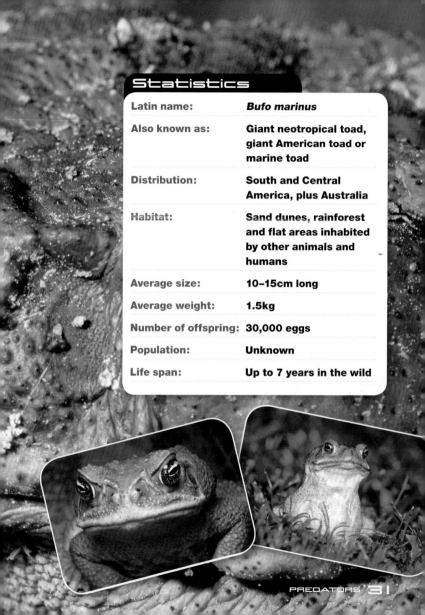

Statistics

Latin name:	*Bufo marinus*
Also known as:	Giant neotropical toad, giant American toad or marine toad
Distribution:	South and Central America, plus Australia
Habitat:	Sand dunes, rainforest and flat areas inhabited by other animals and humans
Average size:	10–15cm long
Average weight:	1.5kg
Number of offspring:	30,000 eggs
Population:	Unknown
Life span:	Up to 7 years in the wild

Cheetah

The spotted cat built for speed

Cheetah

The spotted cat built for speed

Recognisable by their teardrop marks below each eye, cheetahs are the world's fastest land mammal, reaching speeds of over 97kph. With weak jaws and small teeth, they rely on flight rather than fight when hunting. They eat gazelles, impala, springbok and warthogs, but if hunting in packs, they may target wildebeest. Hunting by day, they stalk their prey to within 30m before using their incredible speed to give chase. Although built for speed, cheetahs don't have the stamina to run for long periods of time, so most chases only last about 20 seconds before they give up. If the cheetah gets lucky, it will kill its victim by tripping it during chase and then biting the underside of the throat to suffocate it. However, cheetahs have to keep a look-out to avoid losing their kill to prowling lions and thieving hyenas, since after their chase cheetahs have no energy left to fend off poachers.

Statistics

Latin name:	*Acinonyx jubatus*
Also known as:	**N/a**
Distribution:	**Africa and parts of Asia**
Habitat:	**Deserts, open woodland and savannah**
Average size:	**1.27m long**
Average weight:	**40kg**
Number of offspring:	**1–5 cubs**
Population:	**Approx. 6,700 in the wild**
Life span:	**12–14 years in the wild**

Vampire Bat

The bat with a bloodthirsty appetite

Common
Vampire Bat
The bat with a bloodthirsty appetite

Vampire bats and common vampire bats are the only mammals that feed solely on blood – mainly the blood of large birds, cattle, dogs, pigs and even humans. Mostly described as blood-suckers, they don't actually 'suck' blood from prey, they let it flow from the bite mark before sucking it up, using grooves in their lower lip and tongue as a straw. Their razor-sharp front teeth trim away fur on their prey then cut away at the skin. The bat's saliva contains an anti-coagulant, which is released into the wound, making the blood flow freely rather than clotting. They choose hard-to-reach areas on their victims, such as shoulders or teats. They sometimes return night after night to feed on the same animal, lifting the scab from the previous night's visit to get more blood. They can jump, hop and walk, enabling them to manoeuvre easily around their prey's body. They drink about 20ml of blood a day, and if they don't eat for two days, they usually die.

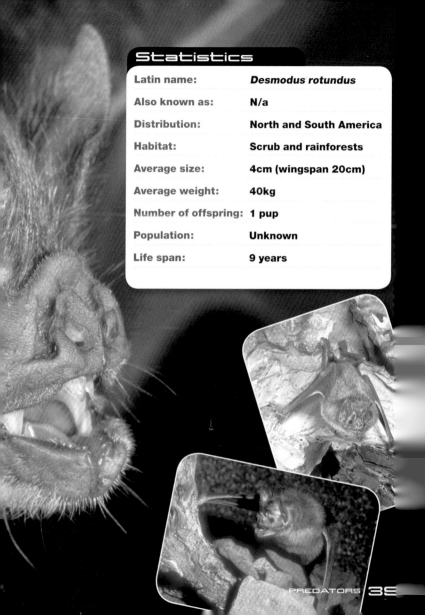

Statistics

Latin name:	*Desmodus rotundus*
Also known as:	N/a
Distribution:	North and South America
Habitat:	Scrub and rainforests
Average size:	4cm (wingspan 20cm)
Average weight:	40kg
Number of offspring:	1 pup
Population:	Unknown
Life span:	9 years

Cougar

The cat with a lethal leap

Cougar

The cat with a lethal leap

Cougars (commonly known as pumas) are the most widespread of the American cats and have the largest distribution of any western hemisphere animal. They also hold the record for the animal with the most names – over 40 in total! Cougars are large, slender cats with incredibly muscular limbs and large feet. These cats hunt mostly deer, moose, birds, squirrels, insects and fish. They are capable of two hunting techniques – stalk-and-ambush and chasing. The stalk-and-ambush method sees the cat stealthily sneak up on its target, then, using its powerful legs, lunge at its prey with a single running jump. It will then leap on the back of its victim before breaking the animal's neck with a forceful bite. They will next drag the body to a safe spot, hiding any leftovers to return to over a period of a few days. Larger prey, such as an elk, will feed a cougar for over a week.

Statistics

Latin name:	*Puma concolor*
Also known as:	Puma, mountain lion, florida panther, red tiger
Distribution:	North and South America
Habitat:	Mountainous regions, forest and grassland
Average size:	1–1.8m long
Average weight:	53–72kg
Number of offspring:	3–4 cubs
Population:	50,000
Life span:	8–13 years

Coyote

The dog whose bite is worse than its bark

Coyote

The dog whose bite is worse than its bark

Their Latin name, *Canis latrans*, means 'barking dog'. They are members of the *Canidae* (dog) family and are a close relative of the grey wolf. Although they live in packs, coyotes usually hunt alone or in pairs. They are largely nocturnal animals, feeding mainly on carrion (dead animals), small animals such as rabbits, squirrels and voles, and also fruit, insects, frogs, snakes and crustaceans. They are opportunistic predators and use a variety of hunting techniques to catch prey. First, they will often track their victim using their keen sense of smell. Next, the coyote will stalk it for about 20 minutes before launching its attack. At other times, they will utilise their speed (during pursuit they can hit speeds of 69kph), giving chase over long distances and finally striking when they have exhausted their victim. They then use their sharp teeth to immobilise their prey by grasping it by the throat and suffocating it.

Statistics

Latin name:	*Canis latrans*
Also known as:	**Prairie wolf, brush wolf**
Distribution:	**Central and North America, Canada and Mexico**
Habitat:	**Open country, woodland, prairies and rural areas**
Average size:	**0.9m long**
Average weight:	**10–20kg**
Number of offspring:	**5–10 pups**
Population:	**50,000**
Life span:	**6–10 years**

Electric
Eel

The most electrifying fish!

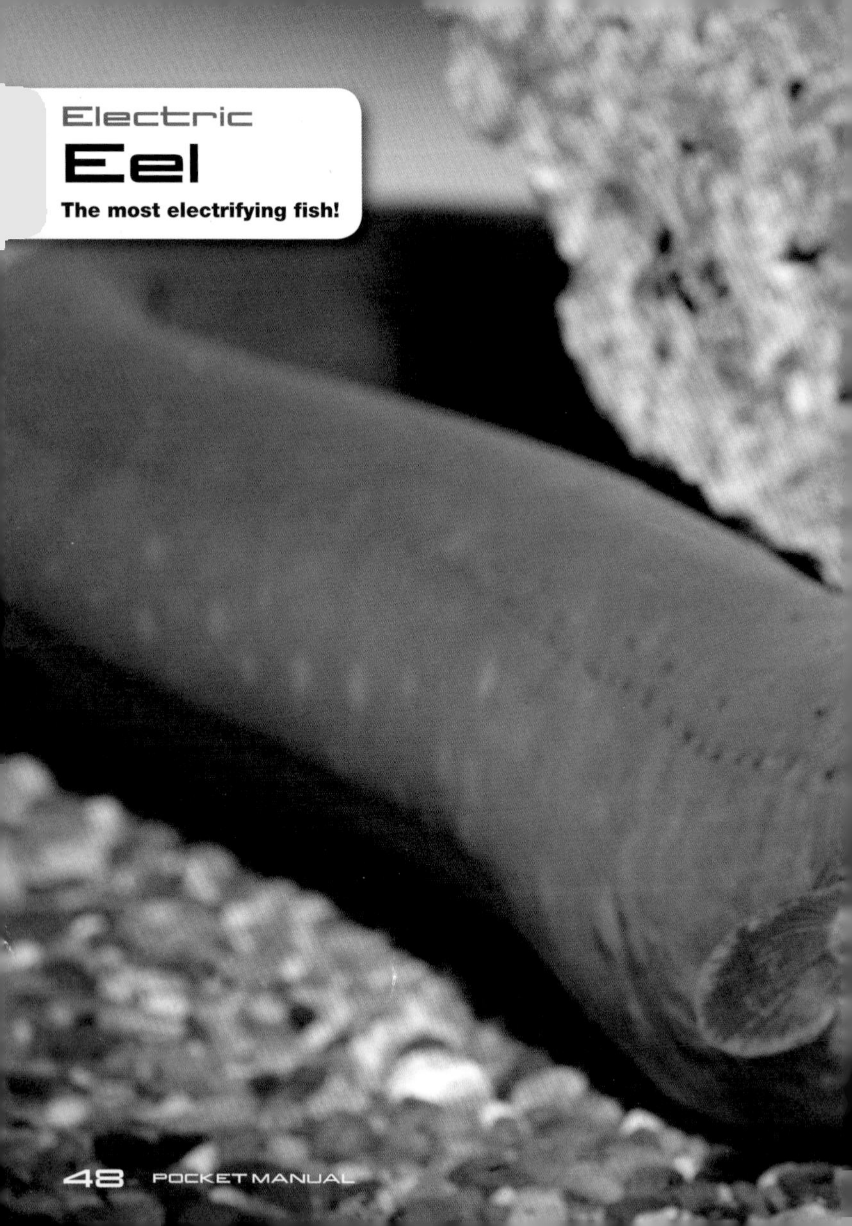

Electric
Eel
The most electrifying fish!

The electric eel isn't actually an eel, but a knifefish – the world's most powerful electric fish. It's found in South American rivers, such as the Amazon, and is a top predator in these waters. They feed mainly on fish and small mammals, but first-born hatchlings will even prey on other eggs and embryos from later batches. It builds up electricity in specifically modified muscles to shock and kill its prey and to use in self-defence. It produces two types of electricity: low voltage is used to find its way around and high voltage is used in predatory attacks to shoot at its prey. It can produce an electric charge of up to 500 volts, which is enough to stun a horse.

Statistics

Latin name:	*Electrophorus electricus*
Also known as:	N/a
Distribution:	South America
Habitat:	Rivers, swamps and creeks
Average size:	2.5m long
Average weight:	20kg
Number of offspring:	Unknown
Population:	Unknown
Life span:	Unknown

Eurasian
Lynx
Europe's quietest yet biggest cat

Eurasian
Lynx
Europe's quietest yet biggest cat

The Eurasian lynx is a medium-sized cat, but the largest of the lynx family. It is also one of the major predators of European and Siberian forests. They are shy, solitary animals that hunt mostly at night. Hares, rabbits, foxes, deer and rodents make up the main part of their diet. Because of their small size, attacking anything much bigger would put the lynx itself at risk. Their habitat is usually rugged forests, which provide plenty of hideouts and stalking opportunities. Eurasian lynx hunt by stalking – sneaking up, then pouncing on their victim. They then make their kill by biting the neck of the animal and severing the spinal cord or suffocating the victim. They often bury uneaten food to return to the next day when they are hungry.

Statistics

Latin name:	*Lynx lynx*
Also known as:	**N/a**
Distribution:	**Europe and Siberia**
Habitat:	**Rugged forests and mountainous areas**
Average size:	**75–100cm long**
Average weight:	**20–25kg**
Number of offspring:	**2 kittens**
Population:	**10,000**
Life span:	**17 years in the wild**

Gila Monster

America's largest lizard

Gila
Monster
America's largest lizard

The Gila monster (pronounced HEE-la) is a carnivorous, venomous lizard – America's largest native lizard. They can also deliver an incredibly poisonous bite. Unlike snakes, the Gila monster injects venom through grooves in the teeth of its lower jaw. Although it only produces a small amount of neurotoxin venom, once it has bitten its victim it will hold on and chew the animal to work as much poison into the wound and the bloodstream as possible. They are largely nocturnal lizards that spend most of their time underground. They feast on small rodents and young birds as well as the eggs of birds and reptiles. They don't often eat big meals, but when they do, they can consume one-third of their body weight! They have excellent smell and hearing, using these to sense ground vibrations of prey in burrows or in vegetation.

Statistics

Latin name:	*Heloderma suspectum*
Also known as:	N/a
Distribution:	America and Mexico
Habitat:	Wet, rocky desert scrub and bush
Average size:	50cm long
Average weight:	1.2kg
Number of offspring:	5–12 eggs
Population:	Unknown
Life span:	20 years

Golden
Eagle
The graceful yet vicious bird of prey

Golden
Eagle
The graceful yet vicious bird of prey

Golden eagles stand apart from other eagles due to their grace, power and agility in flight. These raptors hunt medium-sized mammals, such ass rodents, rabbits, hares and baby deer, plus birds, reptiles and carrion. They can stay in the air for hours at a time and are beautifully graceful when flying. At full speed, they can top 129kph. Their exceptional eyesight lets them spot prey from long distances. Golden eagles soar above the ground, then when they spy food, they will dive down and seize their victim in their curved talons, only using their hooked beaks for tearing flesh from the animal's body. These talons are thought to be more powerful than a human arm or hand! These birds also hunt cooperatively – while one chases its victim to exhaustion towards its partner, the second eagle will swoop in to make the kill.

Statistics

Latin name:	*Aquila chrysaetos*
Also known as:	N/a
Distribution:	Europe, Asia, North Africa and North America but mainly Scottish Highlands
Habitat:	Mountainous areas
Average size:	0.6–1.1m long (wingspan 1.5–2.4m)
Average weight:	3–6kg
Number of offspring:	2 eggs
Population:	Approx. 900 in the UK
Life span:	15–30 years

Golden
Poison Frog

A small but deadly frog

Golden
Poison Frog

A small but deadly frog

The golden poison frog is one of the largest and most deadly of all poison dart frogs. Some tribes in South American rainforests dip their arrows into the golden poison frog's venom to turn them into deadly weapons, which is perhaps where their name came from. This frog may be small but it's the deadliest and could well be the most toxic of all land animals. They carry a poison called 'batrachotoxin'. Just two salt grains' worth of this poison is enough to kill a human, and one wild golden poison frog has enough poison to kill up to 100 adult humans or 20,000 mice! They are deadly to any animal that attempts to eat them. They usually live in groups and are capable of eating animals quite a bit larger than themselves.

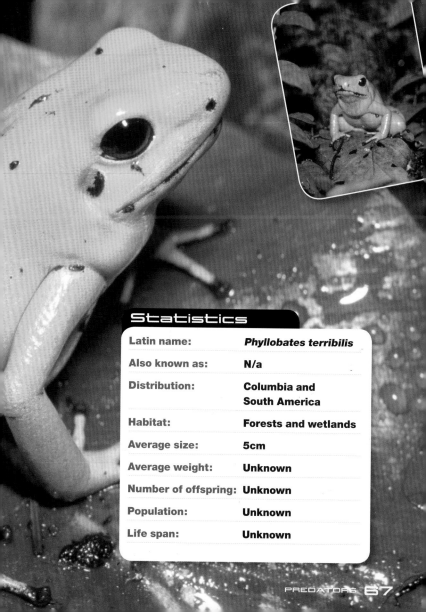

Statistics

Latin name:	*Phyllobates terribilis*
Also known as:	N/a
Distribution:	Columbia and South America
Habitat:	Forests and wetlands
Average size:	5cm
Average weight:	Unknown
Number of offspring:	Unknown
Population:	Unknown
Life span:	Unknown

Goliath Birdeater
Spider
The hairiest predator of them all

Goliath Birdeater
Spider

The hairiest predator of them all

This spider is an arachnid from the tarantula family and is almost certainly the world's largest spider. They live in burrows in the ground and although relatively harmless to humans, their fangs (1–2.5cm long) carry venom and are sharp enough to break through skin. They rely on vibrations in the ground to find prey, as they have poor eyesight. Despite its name, this spider doesn't *usually* feast on birds, instead going for crickets, mealworms, moths and small vertebrates such as frogs, mice and lizards. That said, it is one of the few spiders that can capture and eat a full-grown mouse! They don't use any special techniques when catching prey; instead, they rely on their stealth and strength, sneaking up on their victim and pouncing before inflicting a fatal bite with their venomous fangs. They will then regurgitate digestive juices on to their victims, which in turn break down the prey's soft tissue, allowing the spider to slurp up its meal!

Statistics

Latin name:	*Theraphosa blondi*
Also known as:	N/a
Distribution:	Northern South America
Habitat:	Rain forests and swampy areas
Average size:	30cm leg span
Average weight:	Over 120g
Number of offspring:	100–400 eggs
Population:	Unknown
Life span:	10 years

Great Grey
Owl

The owl with excellent hearing

Great Grey
Owl

The owl with excellent hearing

Arguably the largest of all the owls, the great grey owl is only rivalled by the Eurasian eagle owl and the Blakiston's fish owl. However, this owl's size is down to plumage and fluffy feathers rather than weight! Mostly nocturnal birds, these owls hunt mainly at night, dawn or dusk. They rely heavily on their hearing and visual senses to find prey. They have such acute hearing that they can pick out an animal 60cm beneath snow! When in search of food, they'll either use a perch to sit and wait, or fly through open areas just above the ground watching out for animals. With prey set in its sights, the owl will swoop down, snatching the victim in its sharp talons. Their diet consists of small rodents and voles but also hares, shrews, hawks and ducks. They are carnivores that eat all parts of their prey – anything that can't be digested, like fur and bones, is regurgitated in the form of a pellet.

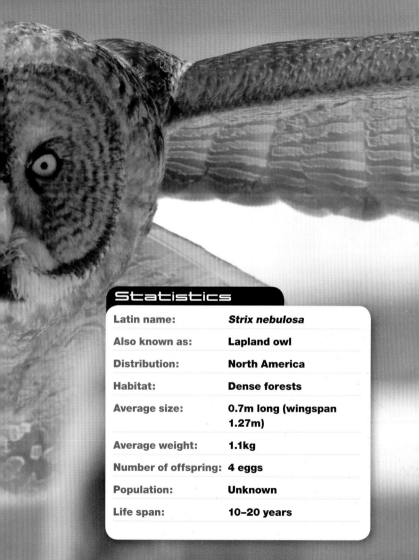

Statistics

Latin name:	*Strix nebulosa*
Also known as:	**Lapland owl**
Distribution:	**North America**
Habitat:	**Dense forests**
Average size:	**0.7m long (wingspan 1.27m)**
Average weight:	**1.1kg**
Number of offspring:	**4 eggs**
Population:	**Unknown**
Life span:	**10–20 years**

Great White
Shark

The most infamous underwater predator

Great White
Shark

The most infamous underwater predator

The great white is the world's most infamous predator and the largest known predatory fish. Growing up to 7m long they can swallow a human whole! They are active swimmers, cruising at 1.6–3.2kph but can hit 40kph when in pursuit of food and can leap straight out of the water to make their kill. They are one of the only sharks known to 'spy-hop', where the shark lifts its head above water to search around for prey. Great whites use an ambush technique for hunting, taking their prey by surprise from below. Most attacks take place just after sunrise, as the darker light makes it hard to see the shark. They hunt fish, including other sharks, seals, small whales, birds and crustaceans. To make their kill, they deliver a disabling bite to their victim, then back off and wait for it to die. Next, the shark will use its serrated teeth as a saw to tear chunks of meat from its prey's body.

Statistics

Latin name:	*Carcharodon carcharias*
Also known as:	Man-eater, death shark or white pointer
Distribution:	Australia, South Africa and Mexico
Habitat:	Mostly temperate coastal and offshore waters
Average size:	4–7m
Average weight:	1,200kg
Number of offspring:	2–12
Population:	Unknown
Life span:	30–40 years

Green
Anaconda
The snake with a deadly hug

Green
Anaconda

The snake with a deadly hug

Anacondas are the one of the world's largest snakes and the green anaconda is the largest member of the boa family. They are aquatic snakes, spending most of their time hunting prey in rivers. To ambush its prey (mainly rodents, fish, birds and reptiles) it lies camouflaged in water, waiting to attack any animal unlucky enough to venture too close to the water. With its eyes and nostrils on top of its head it can stay just under the surface for long periods of time while still being able to see and breathe. To kill, they coil themselves tightly around their prey (called constriction) in a crushing death grip, slowly squeezing their victim to death by suffocation. The snake then devours the animal whole – swallowing it head first so the legs don't get stuck in its throat. Due to a stretchy ligament in their jaw, they can swallow larger animals, too. In one sitting, they can feast on a whole pig or deer.

Statistics

Latin name:	*Eunectes murinus*
Also known as:	Water boa
Distribution:	South America
Habitat:	Dense forests and swampy regions
Average size:	6m long
Average weight:	220kg
Number of offspring:	20–40 young
Population:	Unknown
Life span:	About 30 years

Grey
Wolf

The pack animal that loves a chase

Grey
Wolf

The pack animal that loves a chase

The grey wolf is an ancestor of the domestic dog, found nowadays almost solely in North America. Adaptable creatures, they can live almost anywhere, including urban areas, which has led to them being hunted as they pose a threat to livestock. Grey wolves live and hunt in packs of 2 to 20, feeding on deer, moose, elk, caribou and other hoofed animals. They can run at high speeds for long periods, but to save energy they will often give up and try a different victim. When pack hunting, they cooperate well to bring down larger animals, such as American bison. Their technique is to attack from all sides, targeting the neck and sides of the animal and using their sharp teeth to hold and subdue it. Often, with a big group of prey, grey wolves will initiate a chase and seek out weak, young or elderly victims to attack.

Latin name:	*Canis lupus*
Also known as:	Gray wolf or timber wolf
Distribution:	North America and Canada
Habitat:	Open woodland, tundra and forests
Average size:	1.3–2m long
Average weight:	35–75kg
Number of offspring:	2–10 pups
Population:	Several thousand in the wild
Life span:	8–10 years in the wild

Grizzly
Bear
The bear that likes to grizzle

Grizzly
Bear
The bear that likes to grizzle

After polar bears, grizzly bears (also called brown bears) are the largest land carnivores and are incredibly powerful hunters. Despite their huge size, they can run at 56kph when flat out. They are omnivorous, eating almost anything they can get their paws on. Most grizzly bears feed on rodents, moose, reindeer, sheep and carrion, while Alaskan brown bears make the most of migrating salmon in the rivers. These bears will also readily scavenge and make a meal out of scraps, which has led them into conflict with other animals, such as wolves and even humans. They often stash their food, returning to it at a later date when hungry again. Male bears are impressive diggers, due to their powerfully built shoulders. They use their claws to fight, seek food and mark their territory on the trunks of trees. Although they usually avoid humans, there have been several known attacks.

Statistics

Latin name:	***Ursus arctos horribilis***
Also known as:	**Brown bear, silvertip bear**
Distribution:	**Western North America, East and West Europe and Northern Asia**
Habitat:	**Uplands, dense forests and river valleys**
Average size:	**1.8m–2.1m long**
Average weight:	**95–400kg**
Number of offspring:	**1–4 cubs**
Population:	**Approx. 55,000 in the wild**
Life span:	**20–30 years**

Jaguar

The big cat with a sharp bite

Jaguar
The big cat with a sharp bite

Jaguars are the Americas' largest wild cat. They hunt between dawn and dusk, and their diet consists mainly of deer, tapir, monkeys, fish and livestock. Jaguars actually like water and are very capable swimmers; they have even been known to fish for their food, using their tails as fishing rods, dipping the tip into the water, using it as bait to lure fish within their grasp! When hunting, they kill by biting through their victim's skull between the ears. They have amazingly powerful jaws and sharp canine teeth, which allow them to break through bone and shell – they can even chomp through the shell of animals like the river turtle. After making its kill, the jaguar will then drag the body into dense cover before devouring its prize. They are also excellent tree climbers, so, although most kills are made on the ground, they are capable of climbing trees in order to ambush their prey from above.

Statistics

Latin name:	*Panthera onca*
Also known as:	N/a
Distribution:	South West, South and Central America
Habitat:	Forests, woodland and grassland
Average size:	1.5m long
Average weight:	65kg
Number of offspring:	1–4 cubs
Population:	Unknown
Life span:	11–12 years in the wild

Killer
Whale
The wolf of the sea

Killer
Whale
The wolf of the sea

The killer whale is one of the world's most widespread mammals and one of the fastest animals in the sea, reaching speeds of 56kph. They are also the most dangerous of all the toothed whales, feeding on prey twice the size of themselves. They are top predators of the ocean and prey on marine mammals (whales, seals, sealions), fish, squid and penguins. They hunt in large packs and eat about 220kg of food a day. Killer whales are very sly predators and often sneak up on their victims. Despite their enormous bulk, they can leap on to beaches to kill seals or they find penguins floating on ice sheets, which they nudge off into the sea to devour. Sometimes they chase young whales until exhaustion sets in, and then prevent them returning to the surface to breathe. Seals are often targeted, being head butted or slapped by the killer whale's tail fluke to kill or stun them – disabling or killing their prey before eating, to avoid injury.

Statistics

Latin name:	*Orcinus orca*
Also known as:	Orca, wolf of the sea
Distribution:	Oceans worldwide
Habitat:	Oceans but they prefer temperate waters
Average size:	7–9m
Average weight:	5,000kg
Number of offspring:	1
Population:	50,000
Life span:	40 years

King
Cobra
The snake with a deadly bite

King
Cobra
The snake with a deadly bite

The king cobra is the largest of the venomous land snakes. Its venom is a neurotoxin, which acts specifically on nerve cells and is capable of killing a human or a full-grown Asian elephant! They feed almost entirely on other snakes (*ophiophagus* is Greek for 'snake-eater') and often attack snakes as big as pythons. They smell using their forked tongue, which picks up the scent of nearby prey. They then continually flick their tongue about to gauge the prey's direction. The king cobra poisons its prey through a bite, whereby the venom is forced into the wound through its fangs. Their non-rigid jaws move independently of each other, meaning that the cobra can swallow prey much larger than its head. Although they hunt at all times, after gorging on a large meal, the king cobra may not need to eat again for several months.

Statistics

Latin name:	***Ophiophagus hannah***
Also known as:	**N/a**
Distribution:	**South East Asia**
Habitat:	**Tropical and mountain rain forests**
Average size:	**5.7m long**
Average weight:	**20kg**
Number of offspring:	**20–40 eggs**
Population:	**Unknown**
Life span:	**Up to 22 years**

Komodo
Dragon
The planet's largest lizard

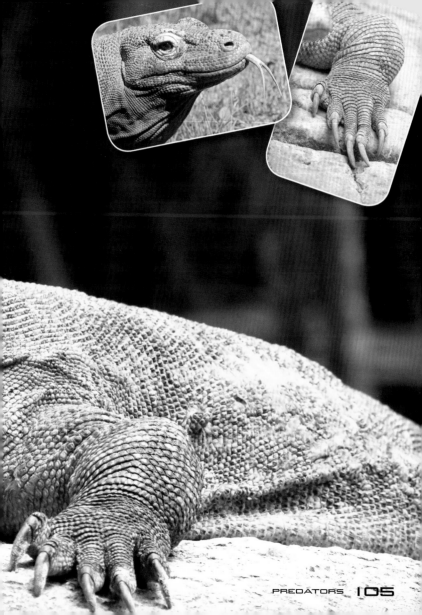

Komodo
Dragon
The planet's largest lizard

The Komodo dragon is also known as the 'land crocodile' and it is the planet's largest lizard. They are excellent runners, swimmers and tree-climbers! They can grow up to 3m long and are ferocious hunters that feast mainly on carrion of pigs and deer, but adult Komodo dragons will eat almost anything they can get their jaws on. They have a poor sense of hearing and rely on their tongue to detect taste and smell – they can detect dead animals up to 5 miles away. When hunting live prey, they use a stealth approach, hiding in long grass and then ambushing the unsuspecting victim. Their powerful serrated teeth rip flesh from their prey, while their flexible lower jaw and skull allow it to swallow big chunks of meat. Komodo dragons may also produce weak venom but possess bacteria in their saliva that can infect and kill its prey even if the

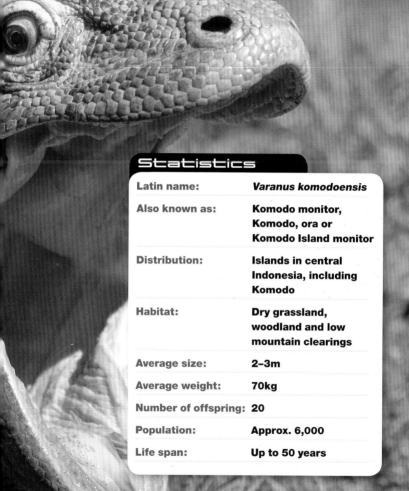

Statistics

Latin name:	*Varanus komodoensis*
Also known as:	Komodo monitor, Komodo, ora or Komodo Island monitor
Distribution:	Islands in central Indonesia, including Komodo
Habitat:	Dry grassland, woodland and low mountain clearings
Average size:	2–3m
Average weight:	70kg
Number of offspring:	20
Population:	Approx. 6,000
Life span:	Up to 50 years

Ladybird

The beetle with a multitude of names

Ladybird

The beetle with a multitude of names

Coccinellidae are a family of beetles commonly known as ladybirds. There are more than 5,000 species worldwide. They are tiny insects measuring about 5mm in size, with a common yellow, orange or red colouring with black spots on their wing covers (different species vary in colour and number of spots). Ladybirds are known as 'gardeners' friends' or 'beneficial predators', as they prey mainly on aphids, scale insects and other garden pests. They even lay their eggs near these insects to ensure their larvae will find the prey more easily. If aphids are scarce, they may also feed on the eggs of moths, beetles, mites and other small insects. If food is completely absent, ladybirds may turn cannibalistic and eat other ladybirds to survive. The larvae and adults patrol plants hunting for insects to eat and some species can consume several hundred aphids per day.

Latin name:	*Coccinellidae*
Also known as:	Lady beetles, ladybugs, lucky bugs or ladybird beetles
Distribution:	Worldwide but most densely in North America and Europe
Habitat:	Plants, vegetable patches, hedgerows and buildings
Average size:	5mm
Average weight:	Unknown
Number of offspring:	10–100
Population:	Unknown
Life span:	2–12 months

Leopard

Top cat of the athletic world

Leopard

Top cat of the athletic world

Leopards are particularly stealthy and agile cats that are very hard to spot, due to their camouflage coats. They are solitary animals (but will aggressively defend their territories) with acute eyesight, the ability to jump 3m in the air and reach speeds of up to 64kph. They are generalist predators and eat more than 90 species of animal, including gazelle, monkeys, wildebeest, snakes and antelope. They are cunning, stealthy hunters that silently stalk their prey until, at the last minute, they pounce! They leap on to their victim, strangling it with one killer bite to the throat. Once it has made its kill, the leopard will drag the body into the safety of the trees, to avoid any unwanted attention from other hungry cats or hyenas. They have incredibly strong jaws and bodies allowing them to lift and drag carcasses three times their own body weight – even up trees!

Statistics

Latin name:	*Panthera pardus*
Also known as:	**N/a**
Distribution:	**India, Africa, China, Siberia and Korea**
Habitat:	**Savannah, forests and jungles**
Average size:	**0.9–1.65m long**
Average weight:	**30–80kg**
Number of offspring:	**2–4 cubs**
Population:	**Unknown**
Life span:	**10–15 years in the wild**

Leopard
Seal
The aggressive aquatic predator

Leopard
Seal

The aggressive aquatic predator

These seals are the second largest species of seal in the Antarctic – their only natural predator is the killer whale. They are bold, powerful, muscular animals, getting their name from their spotty coat but also because they are fearsome hunters. They have excellent sight and smell, which, combined with their streamlined body, makes them top predators in Antarctic waters. Hunting among pack ice, they spend most of their time in the water, feeding on krill, squid, fish and larger animals like king and emperor penguins or crabeater seals. When hunting penguins, they patrol water near ice edges, keeping themselves hidden underwater, waiting for penguins to dive into the sea. They kill the bird by grabbing its feet in their sharp teeth and shaking it violently, beating its body against the surface of the water until it is dead. The leopard seal then flails its prey from side to side in order to rip it into smaller pieces for eating.

Latin name:	*Hydrurga leptonyx*
Also known as:	N/a
Distribution:	Antarctica
Habitat:	Cold waters
Average size:	2.8m
Average weight:	330kg
Number of offspring:	1 pup
Population:	220,000–440,000
Life span:	26 years

Nile
Crocodile
The croc with a toothy smile!

Nile
Crocodile

The croc with a toothy smile!

The Nile crocodile is the top predator of its environment. It's also the second largest species of crocodile and one of the most feared. They have more than 60 teeth, so prey doesn't stand a chance once trapped within this beast's mighty mouth. Although they tend to feast on fish, adult crocodiles will eat almost any vertebrate that wanders too close to the water's edge – even other crocs! They use their body and tail to herd groups of fish towards the bank before eating them with a quick sideways jerk of the head. With their ability to lie half hidden under water and their sprint-speed, these crocs often try their luck attacking larger animals, such as giraffe or buffalo. They'll grab it in their jaws then drag it under water where they'll hold it until it drowns. The Nile crocodile will then rip off and swallow big chunks of flesh by latching on and twisting their bodies – a technique known as the 'death roll'.

Statistics

Latin name:	*Crocodylus niloticus*
Also known as:	**N/a**
Distribution:	**Africa and Madagascar**
Habitat:	**Marshlands, river and lakes**
Average size:	**5m long**
Average weight:	**600kg**
Number of offspring:	**20–80 eggs**
Population:	**50,000–70,000**
Life span:	**70–100 years**

Pacific Electric
Ray
The fish with a nasty shock

Pacific Electric
Ray
The fish with a nasty shock

These fish are certainly deadly! The Pacific electric ray is a species native to the eastern Pacific Ocean. The name comes from the Latin *torpere*, which means to be 'stiffened or paralysed', referring to the effect on someone who handles or steps on a living Pacific electric ray. The electric ray's grey colour (with small black spots) gives it excellent camouflage and makes it hard to distinguish from the sandy ocean bottom. They feed on bony fish, like herrings and halibut. The Pacific electric ray buries itself in mud at the bottom of the sea. When a small fish swims near, the ray sends out a powerful electric charge to stun the fish, allowing it to be eaten with ease rather than with a struggle. This electric charge can reach 50 volts!

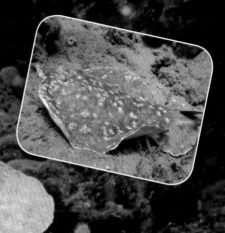

Statistics

Latin name:	*Torpedo californica*
Also known as:	**N/a**
Distribution:	**Gulf of Mexico, California and British Colombia**
Habitat:	**Kelp forests and sandy ocean bottoms**
Average size:	**1.3m long**
Average weight:	**40kg**
Number of offspring:	**Unknown**
Population:	**Unknown**
Life span:	**20 years**

Peregrine
Falcon
The bird that soars higher than the rest

Peregrine
Falcon
The bird that soars higher than the rest

The Peregrine falcon is the fastest of the falcons; in fact, it is the fastest animal on the planet! It is also one of the fiercest avian hunters and successful bird-killers. They almost exclusively feed on birds but have been known to hunt small mammals, including bats and rabbits. If starving, these falcons are known to eat their own chicks! Falcons can't twist and turn while flying flat-out, so instead they dive on prey from above. When in mid-hunting dive (called the stoop), they can reach speeds of over 200kph. They will dive into either wing of their victim, so as not to harm themselves on impact, and then use their talons to stun their prey before carrying it to a safe place to devour.

Statistics

Latin name:	*Falco peregrinus*
Also known as:	**Duck hawk**
Distribution:	**Every continent except Antarctica**
Habitat:	**Mountain ranges, coastlines and river valleys**
Average size:	**36–50cm long (wingspan 100cm)**
Average weight:	**0.5–1.5kg**
Number of offspring:	**2–4 eggs**
Population:	**10,000–100,000**
Life span:	**8–10 years**

Pitcher
Plant

The plant with a deadly sweet side

Pitcher
Plant

The plant with a deadly sweet side

Pitcher plants are carnivorous plants growing in tropical rainforests throughout Sri Lanka. The families *Nepenthaceae* and *Sarraceniaceae* are the best known and most wildly spread groups. In *Nepenthes* pitcher plants, the pitcher (a cup-shaped leaf) grows from the end of tendrils of the pitcher plant, extending from the middle of a leaf, whereas *Sarraceniaceae* grow from the ground upwards. The pitcher's cup-shaped leaves have a sweet liquid in the bottom that attracts insects. This is known as the 'pitfall trap'. Foraging, flying or crawling insects are typical victims. They are lured towards the leaf and then once inside the cup they cannot escape due to the slippery sides and downward-pointing hairs, which make it impossible to climb out. The insect will then drown in the liquid at the bottom and is digested to provide the plant with minerals.

Statistics

Latin name:	*Nepenthes distillatoria*
Also known as:	N/a
Distribution:	Sri Lanka
Habitat:	Waterlogged scrub and cleared areas
Average size:	N/a
Average weight:	N/a
Number of offspring:	N/a
Population:	N/a
Life span:	N/a

Polar
Bear
The king of the Arctic

Polar
Bear
The king of the Arctic

These semi-aquatic marine mammals are the most powerful and aggressive of all the bears. Not only are they the largest land carnivore, but they also have a reputation for being the only animal that actively hunts humans. They are apex predators, meaning they are top of their food chain and have no predators of their own (except humans and larger polar bears). Food wise, they are predominantly carnivorous and hunt seals, small whales, birds, fish and even reindeer. They hunt seals by a process called 'still-hunting'. The bear waits at a seal's breathing hole until the seal surfaces for air. It then breaks through the ice and seizes the seal in its incredibly powerful jaw. They can devour up to 45kg of seal blubber in one go! These bears are exceptional hunters and excellent swimmers, using their huge feet as paddles. They also have a strong sense of smell, and can detect a dead animal from 30km away or a live seal 1m under the ice.

Statistics

Latin name:	*Ursus maritimus*
Also known as:	White bear, sea bear, ice bear or nanuq
Distribution:	The Arctic, Canada, Greenland and Siberia
Habitat:	Land and ice
Average size:	2.4–3m
Average weight:	150–600kg
Number of offspring:	1–3 cubs
Population:	22,000–31,000
Life span:	Up to 25 years

Portuguese
Man O' War

The dangerous ocean organism

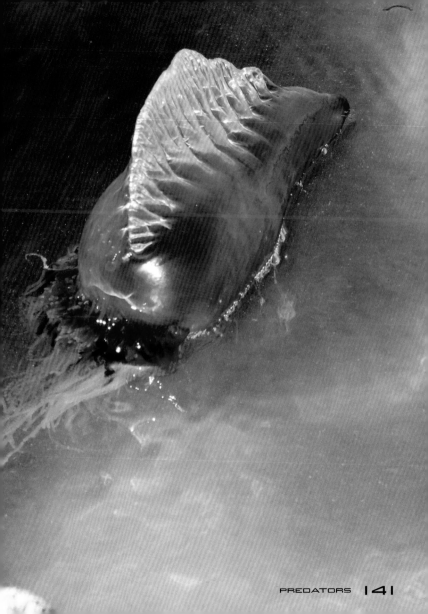

Portuguese
Man O' War

The dangerous ocean organism

Although commonly thought of as a jellyfish, the Portuguese man o' war is actually a siphonophore – rather than being a single animal, it's a colony of four kinds of modified individuals (polyps). Each polyp depends on the others for survival. Portuguese men o' war float in the sea, bobbing along just under the surface with their tentacles dangling downwards. These tentacles can reach 10m in length although the average is 1m. They fish through water, as the muscles in the tentacles contract. They prey on small sea creatures, using poison-filled stinging cells (nematocysts) to sting and kill their victim, before drawing it into the range of the digestive polyps, which then digest it. Prey consists mainly of small crustaceans and other surface plankton. The sting from these tentacles is potentially dangerous to humans and can kill, though it usually only causes extreme pain.

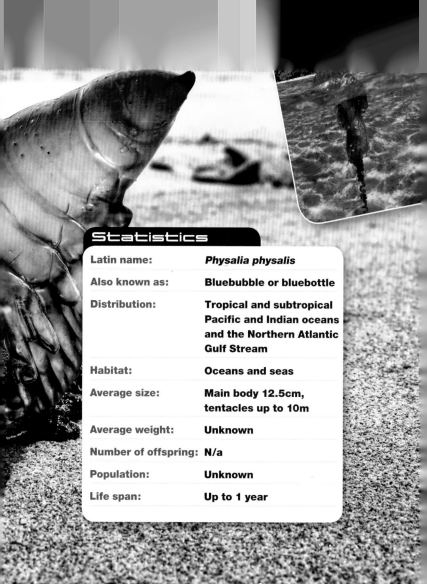

Statistics

Latin name:	*Physalia physalis*
Also known as:	**Bluebubble or bluebottle**
Distribution:	**Tropical and subtropical Pacific and Indian oceans and the Northern Atlantic Gulf Stream**
Habitat:	**Oceans and seas**
Average size:	**Main body 12.5cm, tentacles up to 10m**
Average weight:	**Unknown**
Number of offspring:	**N/a**
Population:	**Unknown**
Life span:	**Up to 1 year**

Praying
Mantis
The ambush predator of the insect world

Praying
Mantis

The ambush predator of the insect world

Praying mantis is the common name for an insect of the Mantodea order – there are more than 2,300 species worldwide – getting its name from its prayer-like stance. They are notorious predators that detect movement of prey by sight using their huge eyes mounted on their triangular head. They have very mobile heads and can turn them 180 degrees, giving them excellent vision and hearing. They also have antennae, which are used for smell. Praying mantids feed through the day and fly by night. They are carnivorous insects and feed on other insects, but occasionally they will also attack small reptiles, mammals and birds. They are ambush predators who are masters of camouflage, using colouring to blend into their surroundings. They then wait for prey to be within stalking distance, before using their raptorial front legs to lash out at incredible speed and quickly snatch their victim before devouring it alive.

Statistics

Latin name:	*Mantis religiosa*
Also known as:	**Praying mantid**
Distribution:	**Worldwide**
Habitat:	**Forests or vegetated areas**
Average size:	**25cm long**
Average weight:	**Unknown**
Number of offspring:	**10–400 eggs**
Population:	**Unknown**
Life span:	**Unknown**

Red
Fox
The UK's number one predator

Red
Fox
The UK's number one predator

Not only is the red fox the most widespread wild carnivore in the world, it is also Britain's number one predator! They are extremely adaptable creatures, which has allowed them to survive in urban areas that are forever encroaching on their usual habitats. Their presence in cities and urban areas is therefore on the increase. They are nocturnal, solitary hunters and opportunist feeders, eating insects, berries, small birds and mammals and any scraps left by humans. They hunt prey by sneaking up on their victim before pouncing on it. Using its 42 powerful teeth, it will then make the kill. There are over 20 million red foxes in the world. Although not a direct human threat, they do viciously attack household pets, livestock and even small children – sometimes for food, other times for fun. They are considered vermin in most urban areas and in England they are culled in an attempt to keep their numbers down.

Statistics

Latin name:	*Vulpes vulpes*
Also known as:	Fox
Distribution:	Across Europe, Canada, USA and Asia
Habitat:	Woodlands, open country and urban areas
Average size:	48–90cm long
Average weight:	4–8kg
Number of offspring:	4–7
Population:	20 million
Life span:	6 years

Red-bellied
Piranha
The remorseless eating machine

Red-bellied
Piranha
The remorseless eating machine

The red-bellied piranha is perhaps the most ferocious fish in the world. They are carnivorous freshwater fish and the red-bellied piranha is renowned for its aggression. From the moment they hatch, they are armed and dangerous. Their teeth are so sharp, in fact, that Amazonians use them as saws and weapons! As they grow older, they venture out in schools of 20 or so fish, using several hunting techniques to kill prey. They often start by surrounding their victims and then eating it alive. They attack with such ferocity that they can strip an animal of its flesh within minutes. Piranhas eat just about anything. Their main diet consists of fish, worms and insects, although they also prey upon sick and weakened animals including humans! Despite their killer bite, they are an important part of their ecosystem, eliminating the weak so that only the strong survive.

Statistics

Latin name:	*Pygocentrus nattereri*
Also known as:	Red piranha
Distribution:	South America
Habitat:	Rivers
Average size:	15–25cm long
Average weight:	3.5kg
Number of offspring:	Several clutches of eggs
Population:	Unknown
Life span:	Unknown

Red-tailed
Hawk
A red-tailed predator of the sky

Red-tailed
Hawk
A red-tailed predator of the sky

The red-tailed hawk is a large bird of prey found mainly throughout North America and Canada. When in flight, they flap their wings as little as possible to save energy. They reach fantastic speeds and can soar up to 64kph, but when diving they can hit speeds of 193kph! These hawks usually use a 'sit and wait' hunting technique. They'll find a perch and wait, putting their keen eyesight to use in detecting even the smallest movement in the grass below. Once they've spotted potential prey, they will swoop down, snatching the victim in their viciously sharp talons. One other hunting method that red-tailed hawks use is patrolling open areas in flight, flying only a few metres off the ground in search of food. They feast mainly on small mammals, reptiles and birds; however, when near water they will also feed on fish.

Statistics

Latin name:	*Buteo jamaicensis*
Also known as:	Chickenhawk
Distribution:	North America, Canada and the West Indies
Habitat:	Open country with high perches
Average size:	0.5m long (wingspan 1.2m)
Average weight:	1.4kg
Number of offspring:	1–3 eggs
Population:	2 million
Life span:	10–20 years

Short-tailed
Stingray

The fish with a sting in its tail

Short-tailed
Stingray
The fish with a sting in its tail

The short-tail stingray is the world's largest stingray. They often have two stings, which bear toxin glands. They have long, flexible tail spines containing saw-edged venomous spikes. When threatened, these are injected into the stingray's victim with huge force. They have eyes on top of their bodies, meaning they cannot see their prey, so instead they swim with synchronised wing flaps to stir up sand-bed sediment and victims. They also use their sense of smell and electro-receptors to locate prey. They feed mostly on molluscs, crustaceans, small fish and invertebrates. Their mouths on the bottom of their body have powerful shell-crushing teeth, so once they've located their prey, they place it in their mouths before crushing it to death. The short-tail stingray made its name in 2006 as the stingray that killed the world-famous TV naturalist Steve Irwin, by spearing him through the heart.

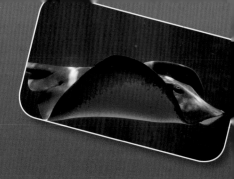

Latin name:	*Dasyatis brevicaudata*
Also known as:	Smooth stingray, bull ray
Distribution:	Africa, Australia and New Zealand
Habitat:	Tropical coastal waters
Average size:	4.3m
Average weight:	330kg
Number of offspring:	5–10
Population:	Unknown
Life span:	Unknown

Siberian
Tiger

A big cat with an even bigger appetite

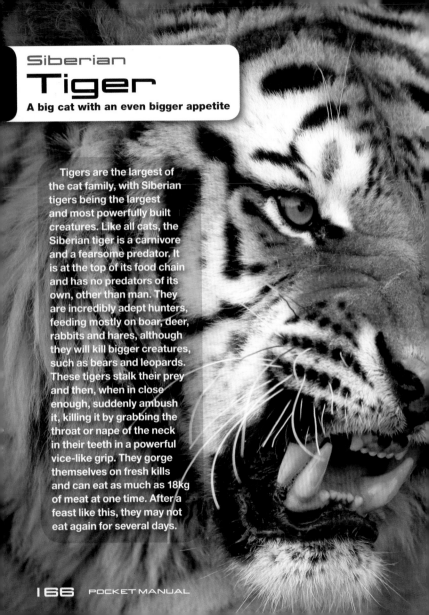

Siberian
Tiger
A big cat with an even bigger appetite

Tigers are the largest of the cat family, with Siberian tigers being the largest and most powerfully built creatures. Like all cats, the Siberian tiger is a carnivore and a fearsome predator. It is at the top of its food chain and has no predators of its own, other than man. They are incredibly adept hunters, feeding mostly on boar, deer, rabbits and hares, although they will kill bigger creatures, such as bears and leopards. These tigers stalk their prey and then, when in close enough, suddenly ambush it, killing it by grabbing the throat or nape of the neck in their teeth in a powerful vice-like grip. They gorge themselves on fresh kills and can eat as much as 18kg of meat at one time. After a feast like this, they may not eat again for several days.

Statistics

Latin name:	*Panthera tigris altaica*
Also known as:	**North China tiger, Manchurian, Amur or Korean tiger**
Distribution:	**Russian Far East**
Habitat:	**Forests**
Average size:	**3m long**
Average weight:	**220kg**
Number of offspring:	**1–4 cubs**
Population:	**Approx. 3,900 in the wild**
Life span:	**12–13 years**

Spotted Hyena

The animal that loves to laugh

Spotted
Hyena
The animal that loves to laugh

Spotted hyenas are the largest of the hyena family. They have a reputation for being cowardly scavengers, but they are actually incredibly clever, skilful hunters. Spotted hyenas hunt medium-sized hoofed animals but often attack animals much bigger than themselves, such as buffalo and zebra. They have enormous appetites and can eat one-third of their body weight in one meal! Their immensely powerful jaws and teeth allow them to crush animal bones and feed on the marrow inside. They also have special stomach acids, meaning they can feed on parts of dead animals that would otherwise just rot inside them. When hunting larger animals, they hunt in packs, taking down the prey by biting it and dragging it to the ground. They are built for endurance and can chase at 48kph for over 3km without tiring. All hyenas are renowned for their high-pitched cackle, which makes them sound as if they are laughing!

Statistics

Latin name:	*Crocuta crocuta*
Also known as:	**Laughing hyena**
Distribution:	**East, West and Southern Africa**
Habitat:	**African savannahs and fringes of desert, and tropical rainforests**
Average size:	**1.3–1.85m**
Average weight:	**45–70kg**
Number of offspring:	**1–2 cubs**
Population:	**Unknown**
Life span:	**10–20 years in the wild**

Tasmanian Devil

The marsupial with a killer munch

Tasmanian Devil
The marsupial with a killer munch

The Tasmanian devil is the largest carnivorous marsupial in the world. Early European settlers called it 'The Devil', due to its spine-chilling screeches and bad temper! They are nocturnal marsupials well known for their size (of a small dog but more muscular), strong odour, loud screeching and viciousness when eating. They have long whiskers on their face, which help them to locate prey when foraging at night. When hunting for food, they amble slowly but can gallop very quickly if giving chase. If considering bite force relative to body size, the Tasmanian devil has the strongest bite of any living mammal! They can kill mammals the size of sheep, though their favourite meal is wombats. They are opportunistic eaters, feeding on most small mammals and will scavenge carrion, too. When they eat, they devour everything (including internal organs) using their powerful teeth to tear through fur and break bones. They eat approximately 15 per cent of their body weight a day.

Statistics

Latin name:	*Sarcophilus harrisii*
Also known as:	**The Devil**
Distribution:	**Tasmania**
Habitat:	**Forests, woodlands and urban areas of Tasmania**
Average size:	**0.65m long**
Average weight:	**8kg**
Number of offspring:	**20–30 young**
Population:	**20,000–50,000**
Life span:	**Approx. 6 years**

Tiger
Shark

The ocean trash can

Tiger
Shark

The ocean trash can

This fearsome shark is nicknamed the 'dustbin of the sea' due to its relentless appetite and ability to eat anything in its path! They have excellent eyesight but rely mainly on their acute sense of smell to detect prey. Tiger sharks are also incredibly fast swimmers, reaching speeds of 32kph. They have flat, triangular, serrated teeth, strong enough to bite through bone and turtle shells. Their meals mainly include turtles, seabirds, fish, seals, sea snakes and other sharks, although trainers, backpacks and a suit of armour are just a few of the things that have been found inside a tiger shark's stomach! They are extremely aggressive sharks and have been known to circle their prey, prodding it with their snout, before attacking. When eating, this shark devours every last piece of its victim, leaving nothing behind. They are ferocious killers and a danger to animals and humans – they come second to great whites in the record-holding stakes for attacks on humans!

Statistics

Latin name:	*Galeocerdo cuvier*
Also known as:	N/a
Distribution:	Worldwide but especially the Pacific
Habitat:	Warm, tropical oceans and seas
Average size:	3–4m long
Average weight:	600kg
Number of offspring:	10–80 pups
Population:	Unknown
Life span:	15–20 years

Venus
Flytrap
The plant with a lethal trap

Venus
Flytrap
The plant with a lethal trap

The Venus flytrap is the most commonly known carnivorous plant, which catches and digests insects and arachnids by trapping them in its leaves. The edges of its leaves have teeth-like protrusions called cilia. Inside, the leaves are bright pink in an attempt to lure passing insects. The inside leaf also has trigger hairs. If an insect stumbles against these, the 'trapping' mechanism is activated and the leaf starts to close, with the prey inside. The hairs must be touched twice in quick succession to let the plant know that it is prey rather than drops of rain triggering the mechanism. Once trapped inside, the leaves lock together forming a 'stomach' in which digestive juices are released to kill the insect and digestion occurs. The Venus flytrap closes its trap within 100 milliseconds, but it takes approximately 10 days to open again, after digestion.

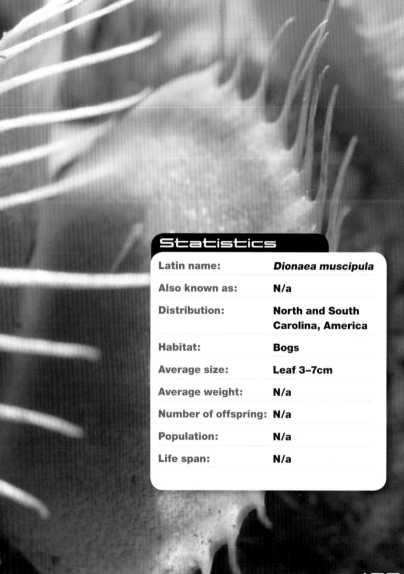

Statistics

Latin name:	*Dionaea muscipula*
Also known as:	N/a
Distribution:	**North and South Carolina, America**
Habitat:	**Bogs**
Average size:	**Leaf 3–7cm**
Average weight:	N/a
Number of offspring:	N/a
Population:	N/a
Life span:	N/a

Whip
Scorpion

The invertebrate with a killer crush

Whip
Scorpion
The invertebrate with a killer crush

The whip scorpion is not a true scorpion, rather an invertebrate belonging to the Arachnida class and the order of Uropygi. The name 'uropygid' means 'tail rump' referring to the thin whip-like projection from the end of the scorpion. They have no sting in their tail but have glands near their abdomen which, when threatened, spray a vinegar-smelling substance. They have eight legs but use only six for walking – the front two work as antennae-like sensory organs. The whip scorpion has two large pincers at the front, with one pair of eyes at the front of its head and three on each side. Their flat bodies allow them to squeeze into narrow crevices and nooks. They are carnivorous and hunt mostly at night, when they prey on small arthropods, worms and slugs. When they locate prey, they move in for the kill, fatally crushing their victim (before tearing it apart) between special 'teeth' found on the inside of the front legs.

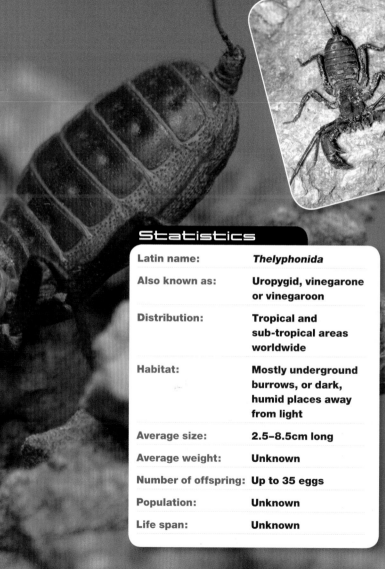

Statistics

Latin name:	*Thelyphonida*
Also known as:	**Uropygid, vinegarone or vinegaroon**
Distribution:	**Tropical and sub-tropical areas worldwide**
Habitat:	**Mostly underground burrows, or dark, humid places away from light**
Average size:	**2.5–8.5cm long**
Average weight:	**Unknown**
Number of offspring:	**Up to 35 eggs**
Population:	**Unknown**
Life span:	**Unknown**

Checklist

 American Alligator
Date   Location

 American Black Vulture
Date   Location

 Asiatic Lion
Date   Location

 Black Widow Spider
Date   Location

 Box Jellyfish
Date   Location

 Cane Toad
Date   Location

 Cheetah
Date   Location

 Common Vampire Bat
Date   Location

Cougar
Date   Location

Coyote
Date **Location**

Electric Eel
Date **Location**

Eurasian Lynx
Date **Location**

Gila Monster
Date **Location**

Golden Eagle
Date **Location**

Golden Poison Frog
Date **Location**

Goliath Birdeater Spider
Date **Location**

Great Grey Owl
Date **Location**

Great White Shark
Date **Location**

Green Anaconda
Date **Location**

Grey Wolf
Date **Location**

Grizzly Bear
Date **Location**

Jaguar
Date **Location**

Killer Whale
Date **Location**

King Cobra
Date **Location**

Komodo Dragon
Date **Location**

Ladybird
Date **Location**

Leopard
Date **Location**

Leopard Seal
Date **Location**

Nile Crocodile
Date **Location**

Pacific Electric Ray
Date **Location**

Peregrine Falcon
Date **Location**

Pitcher Plant
Date **Location**

Polar Bear
Date **Location**

Portuguese Man O' War
Date   Location

Praying Mantis
Date   Location

Red Fox
Date   Location

Red-bellied Piranha
Date   Location

Red-tailed Hawk
Date   Location

Short-tailed Stingray
Date   Location

Siberian Tiger
Date   Location

Spotted Hyena
Date   Location

Tasmanian Devil
Date   Location

Tiger Shark
Date   Location

Venus Flytrap
Date   Location

Whip Scorpion
Date   Location

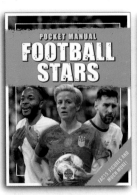

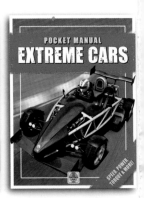